Praise for *Camouflage to Pinstripes*

"Timely, motivating, life-changing message—this book is essential reading."

—General Gary E. Luck
US Army (Ret)

"We have needed a book like this for a long time. Spread the word—buy it, share it, gift it to a friend. This book will optimistically change the way you think about life after the military. A must-read for transitioning military but also for those hiring from this extremely qualified workforce."

—Major General Gordon C. Nash
US Marine Corps (Ret)
Corporate VP, Sierra Nevada Corporation

"In a brilliant, practical way, Dr. Savion answers many of the most frequently asked questions about making a change from military to civilian life. This is a great resource for anyone wishing to effectively start anew."

—Dr. Michael J. Marquardt
Best-selling author, *Leading with Questions: How Leaders Find the Right Solutions by Knowing What to Ask*

"*Camouflage to Pinstripes* is the perfect blend of academic wisdom, voices of experience, and practical advice for successfully transitioning from military to civilian life. Having lived the experience, Dr. Savion is the perfect guide."

—Lynette A. Pujol, PhD
Psychologist, behavioral medicine and military population resiliency

Camouflage
to
Pinstripes

Camouflage
to
Pinstripes

Learning to Thrive in Civilian Culture

DR. SYDNEY M. SAVION

Brown Books Publishing Group
Dallas, Texas

Camouflage to Pinstripes
Learning to Thrive in Civilian Culture

Brown Books Publishing Group
16250 Knoll Trail, Suite 205
Dallas, Texas 75248
www.brownbooks.com
(972) 381-0009

ISBN: 978-1-61254-033-7
Library of Congress Control Number: 2011942861

Printed in the United States of America
10 9 8 7 6 5 4 3 2 1

In honor of the institution of the armed forces and the men and women who serve therein, the author has chosen to capitalize names of the branches of the military.

For more information, please visit www.CamouflageToPinstripes.com.

To the Soldiers, Sailors, Airmen, and Marines who
watch over this nation and preserve the very freedom
I have enjoyed while penning this book.

Contents

Acknowledgments xiii

Preface xvii

1. **This Process is a Journey:** Life Transition, Part One 1

2. **How I See Myself:** Life Transition, Part Two 17

3. **Reality Has Struck:** Changes in Culture 33

4. **A Major Paradigm Shift:** Identity and Purpose 47

5. **Go Out and Get It:** Growth and Support 59

6. **Improvise, Adapt, and Overcome:** Self-Renewal 71

About the Author

Acknowledgments

In memory of my beloved mother, Jacquelyn, who never failed me and who, with every loving breath, secured my place on this earth to live out God's plan and purpose for my life.

Special thanks to my sister, Tiffany (here's to the Mickey Mouse watch days); Delores, my forever friend; Bryan, who inspired me to share these insights; Brown Books Publishing Group, for seeing the value and possibilities; all who touched and provided services in support of this book; the many (too many to thank by name) who graciously joined me, walked alongside of me, helped me along life's journey, and shaped my way of thinking about the human experience and meaningful contribution. Most of all, my sempiternal gratitude to God—thank you for your love and grace.

Two roads diverged in a wood, and I—
I took the one less traveled by,
and that has made all the difference.
—Robert Frost

Preface

If you are reading this book, I imagine you are either thinking about getting out of the military, considering retiring, or have already retired. My guess is that you are probably reading this book because you are still searching for a checklist, signposts, or a simple understanding of the steps you need to take to successfully assimilate into the civilian way of life. Because let's face it: the culture, the life, and the institution of the military are anything but mainstream. A plethora of books are available to give you tips and guidance on career transition, new employment, writing a résumé, enhancing your employability, and finding a job. This major life change, however, is much more than a change in profession, relocating to another assignment, or rearranging furniture in a new house. This book provides you with a glimpse into the psychological process you are experiencing or will experience beyond simply doffing a camouflage uniform and donning a pinstriped suit.

ABOUT THIS BOOK

This book is intended to heighten your awareness about the mental and emotional struggle you will face as a result of this change in culture and to provide insights for traversing the process of surrendering the old life situation and starting anew. There is no doubt that you have faced many changes in your lifetime because change is unending—before you depart this earth you will face many more. What I hope to help you understand is that when you exit the military and return to civilian culture, you are exchanging social structures that run counter to one another. In essence, you are exchanging a structured culture for an unstructured culture.

I am sure you have either heard stories of or personally know individuals who found it very difficult to deal with the magnitude of differences that came with civilian culture. Some of these individuals continually expressed dissatisfaction with the civilian way of life, turned to drugs, committed crimes, were unable to hold a steady job, incited stress and fissure in their family, or perhaps even committed suicide. On the other hand, there are stories that reflect deep-rooted challenges in which individuals were able to demonstrate strength of mind, body, and spirit and by all accounts successfully navigate this new life situation.

Individuals often find that they are not well prepared for the journey they need to undertake in civilian culture. There are many reasons for the difficulties. Some experts point to this change occurring at midlife; others point to the combination of the military social structure and the individual's deep inculcation in that way of life over a period of decades. Upon an individual's return to civilian culture, one thing is paramount to achieving a positive outcome: to mentally and emotionally surrender the old situation and experiment and grow comfortable with new ways of being, doing, thinking, and engaging with a new environment. These processes may be counterintuitive. If you take nothing else away from this book, I hope you come to understand that you must arrive at a place in your mind that will allow you to experience the complementarity and coexistence of yourself with civilian culture. This book will offer you insights to orient you from the inside out. This is your book of signposts on effectively starting anew in civilian culture.

Here are four guiding precepts:

- Recognize that life transition is a gradual psychological process, not a static event.
- Be deliberate in surrendering the past.
- Recognize that life is going to be somewhat chaotic for a while.
- Visualize the future you desire to have.

ASSUMPTIONS

In this book, I make several assumptions about you, the reader:

- You do not know everything you need to know about how to successfully become comfortable with this change.
- You are interested in finding out what to expect upon your return to civilian culture.
- You want to be as successful in civilian culture as you were in military culture.

- You want to be optimally prepared for your departure from military culture.
- You are ready to develop a plan of action and effectively execute it.

Two Roads

Some of you may have intentionally declined (or "taken a rain check on") the path of employment as a Department of Defense (DoD) contractor or government civilian, instead choosing the less common path of those joining the ranks of corporate America, academia, or some other non-DoD establishment that generally has a significantly different organizational structure, subculture, and code of conduct, as well as significantly different values and conversations than the military.

It is widely known that it is easier to be presented with an opportunity to doff your uniform and don a pair of khakis and a polo shirt and resume a semblance of the job you were doing—now as a DoD contractor or government civilian— almost the very next day. It is easier to settle into a familiar environment with people who are generally fellow military comrades with familiar organizational values, missions, and culture. The environment is fairly safe (perhaps not risk-free, but there is limited risk), offers structure, is noncompetitive, and is similar to that which you became habituated to in the military, much unlike corporate America or academia. On the other hand, deliberately choosing to seek employment outside of the DoD and embracing a different lifestyle, including a shift in habits, attitudes, tastes, social standards, and economic level, is considered to be an anomaly among individuals who retire from the military. This is truly the road less traveled.

Real Research

For individuals changing from military to civilian culture, sociologist Dr. James Dowd of the University of Georgia found that those choosing not to completely disconnect from the military may experience a heightened challenge in coping with the career and lifestyle change they face in civilian society. The individual now living in civilian society who has retired from the military has faced a group of boundary crossings: "Soldiers leaving active duty after careers that last between twenty and thirty years are not only crossing over from the status of worker to that of a retiree, they are also making what for some is [a] far more problematic shift from the military to civilian society. No longer in uniform, no longer in this communal society governed by special regulations, a unique code of conduct, and [a] traditional set of cultural values, they enter the larger world of autonomous, atomistic, rationally individualistic civilians."

Dowd offers resounding insights, but I found context is the huge differentiator on the journey of coping with a life transition of this magnitude. I found the term "completely" to be relative, because after having given twenty to thirty years of one's life in service of something greater than oneself—in this case serving in the military in defense of this nation—there are remnants, friendships, and memories of that life that are forever embedded within ourselves. We only need to ask World War II and Vietnam veterans if they have completely disconnected from the military. Even when individuals are intentional about "wholly" disconnecting, they experience the challenges of coping with a new career and lifestyle. These challenges are heightened during the time of questioning in which the individual begins to sort out and try to understand him- or herself in relation to his or her environment as a result of experiencing a culture change.

Some of you will choose or have already chosen a more convenient and familiar path in civilian culture that aligns more closely with the life you grew accustomed to in the military. Rather than traveling that path, others of you will instead choose or have already chosen to take a path of new vistas, of discovery, of stretching yourselves mentally and emotionally—a path of the unknown. When you come to this point in your life where two roads diverge, you can choose either path. If you choose to take the path less traveled, though, I believe that will make all the difference in your life-transitioning experience and in the manner in which you are able to launch into civilian culture and start anew.

INFORMATION BARS USED IN THIS BOOK

Throughout the text of this book, you will find several helpful information bars between paragraphs that can make your journey easier.

- A **Key** bar indicates key information and strategic actions you need to consider in order to successfully traverse the life transition process (*take action*).

- A **Heads-Up** bar indicates a heads-up factor for something you need to watch out for (*be aware*).
- A **Real Research** bar indicates real research—findings that have emerged from scholarly studies (*learn*).
- A **Real People** bar represents real people and real-life experiences of those who have made a successful life transition (*connect*). Note: pseudonyms have been used for these narratives, which represent all services (Army, Air Force, Navy, and Marines).

GETTING FROM HERE TO THERE

Chapters 1 and 2 provide a discussion of the life transition process; chapters 3, 4, and 5 cover in detail various aspects of the process, such as culture, identity, purpose, growth, and support; and chapter 6 discusses the eventual goal of self-renewal. You don't necessarily need to read this book from cover to cover—you can begin with whatever chapter resonates with you. If you are not familiar with the concept of life transition from a psychological perspective, you may want to start with the first two chapters. Also, be sure to follow the references and helpful illustrations strategically placed throughout the text to clarify key points. Now that you have a copy of this book, you will experience a growing understanding of this journey from camouflage to pinstripes.

I hope this book will not only enrich your life but will also generate dialogue in your community, dialogue that will foster an appreciation of the life-transitioning experience of an invaluable yet often overlooked segment of our culture—you, the Soldier, Sailor, Airman, and Marine!

All changes, even the most longed for, have their melancholy;
for what we leave behind us is a part of ourselves;
we must die to one life before we can enter another.
—Anatole France

Chapter One

This Process is a Journey:
Life Transition, Part One

If you are like many who exit the military and return to civilian culture, this major life change may set off an emotional and cognitive struggle, especially if you have dedicated more than half your adult life to military service. Emotionally, the event may arouse a myriad of feelings that may run counter to your comfort zone. Cognitively, the event may impinge on your conscious way of thinking, learning, and, quite frankly, your deep-rooted modus operandi. This major life change may even make you experience the sensation of the weight of the world caving in on you.

There are two principal reasons why this major life change generates strife:
- Culture
- Life transition

Individuals who retire from the military tend not to find a similar life in civilian culture. Neither society nor most individuals are aware of, let alone place a high emphasis on, the implications of life transition that result from such a major life change. Hence, unbeknownst to you, you may find that you are ill-equipped when a change of this kind occurs, be it planned or unplanned. Moreover, on entry into military service, an individual undergoes a socialization process that shapes and guides his or her behavior to assimilate as part of a cohesive unit. It would stand to reason that when an individual exits military service and returns to civilian culture, resocialization must occur. Herein lies the challenge. Unlike the process employed by the military to socialize you into the institution, there is no formal civilian resocialization process. No elaborate resettlement system has been established, nor are there frequent signs along the way to help orient you to civilian culture.

Heads-Up

It is up to you to resocialize yourself and make yourself fit for living in civilian culture. This is often taken for granted. What you may not know or recognize is that in order to achieve successful resocialization, you must be retrained mentally and emotionally to become comfortable with functioning in a different culture.

The bottom line: the cultural socialization taken together with the psychological process you will undergo constitutes a riveting, major life change. You need to be aware that as a result of exiting the military and returning to civilian culture, you will also undergo a life transition process that will affect all aspects of your daily life.

This segues into understanding the no-kidding theory that underlies the journey "from camouflage to pinstripes." That theory is this: life transition is more than a physical transformation; it is a psychological progression of experiences that will accompany you upon exiting the military and returning to civilian culture. In all likelihood, you will not sense a clear demarcation in this psychological progression of emotionally and mentally shedding your camouflage, moving forward through a puzzling state, reorienting, and ultimately donning your pinstripes to start your life anew. Where one state ends and another begins is not formulaic. Rather—it is fluid and unfolds in a sloping and overlapping manner sometimes gently or not so gently, depending on the energy you infuse in the process.

———— Heads-Up ————

The process of this change is gradual, and you may discover that you experience a sense of both disorientation and reorientation all at once. You are not alone; almost everyone experiences unsettling periods of time when they embark on an epic, life-altering journey, whether personally or professionally.

The last point regarding why you may tend to struggle with this major life change is something called adult life course. Those of you who have spent decades (yes, decades) in the military are not returning to the civilian culture you once knew as young adults. Given this, many of my readers may be considered middle-aged, and *Camouflage to Pinstripes* will address the specific challenges you will face. However, some of my readers may be older or younger—and this book also offers invaluable guidance for you as well.

———— Real Research ————

Studies conducted by Dr. Bernice Neugarten, an authority on aging, found that unlike during the self-consciousness of your youth, when you are middle-aged you tend to be introspective, conscious of self-reappraisal, and better able take inventory of your place in life. This means you are prone to be preoccupied with your inner world rather than the outer world, and your readiness to attach to activities and persons in your environment is decreasing.

However, my own findings have slightly deviated in this regard. When people cultivate a growing awareness and engage in self-reflection, they experience an increase in emotional energy toward themselves, others, and their environment.

Chapters 2 and 3 provide further insights on the topics of life transition and culture. These chapters will help you make sense of your lived experience and provide you with a better understanding of how to effectively attend to your life transition now or long before you retire from the military and return to civilian culture.

———— Real People ————

Winston
"As I reflect upon this whole experience, it seems to me that there were several parts of my life that were affected by the

life transition experience. I found that I had to adjust mentally, emotionally, and physically. I see my life in stages. When I look at it, I know that from the beginning of my life up through college I pretty much lived my life to live. I mean, I wanted to have fun and did not have a lot of worries, so I just lived life—I got up every morning and simply enjoyed life.

"Then I entered the military, and for the next twenty-eight years I found myself totally absorbed with a profession that I was absolutely in love with and realized that I was actually living my life to work. I got up every day with the intent of going and doing the best I could at work because I truly loved and believed in what I was doing. I believed in the mission and in taking care of soldiers and their families, and that is what was most important to me.

"When I retired from the military, I went through this period where I had to adjust to a new reality in which I was working to live as opposed to living to work. I enjoy what I'm doing now, but quite frankly I am performing this job as a vice president and senior executive of a corporation in order for me to maintain a certain lifestyle."

UNDERSTANDING LIFE TRANSITION

First of all, life transition is not the same as change. While the two converge, life transition reflects a gradual psychological progression. In essence, you will experience a period of time when you feel a heightened level of ambiguity in your situational awareness—perhaps better understood as being in a fog. This will eventually give way to clarity as you internalize and come to grips with a new life situation. Moreover, life transition is natural as it is transformative. You will discover that this process morphs you in a very compelling way from the inside out. Change, simply put, is an occurrence—in this instance, your departure from the military and return to civilian culture. As you probably well know, both life transition and change are a constant in adult life.

———— Real Research ————

Life transition is described by Dr. William Bridges as a psychological process, an inner reorientation and self-redefinition that an individual goes through in order to incorporate marker events into his or her life. Marker events often have momentous impact upon and change a person's life situation in such a way that it demands that a person cope and adjust. Also informing this point of view are the works of the good Dr. Frederic M. Hudson, a renowned expert in adult change. He viewed life transition as a natural process of renewal of the inner self, which leads to renewal of the outer self and the discovery of inner resources that contain immense value and direction for how to live. Moreover, he offers, it is renewal of the inner self that unfolds in a cyclical manner and consists of periods of change an individual goes through in order to incorporate marker events into his or her life.

While life transition is triggered by a marker event and naturally unfolds in three multidimensional states—what I call "questioning," "seeking," and "starting anew"—individuals need to be introspective and deliberate about taking control of their lives. "Being intentional" is a call to action for individuals to shape and direct their thoughts and deeds in purposeful ways that will improve their comfort level with the new environment and situation, leverage their resources to achieve success, and promote a healthy outlook on their lives. So awaken and repurpose your skills and talents to contribute to society in a different and meaningful way. Choose the life you desire to live, visualize yourself living it, step into your new environment with high intention, and actualize it as you press toward the ultimate aim of self-renewal. If you have lived by the mantra "failure is not an option," then you need to think and act as though success *is*!

———————— Key ————————

Life transition must occur to attain self-renewal. It is essential that you embrace change, be intentional about reshaping your identity, cultivate awareness, and recognize that self-renewal begins from the inside out. Ultimately, the journey is for you to arrive at a place in your life in which you have disconnected from the old life situation and connected comfortably to the new.

———————— Real Research ————————

We learned from Dr. Bridges's extensive research and observations of his own life and the lives of others that life transition is psychological and not simply another word synonymous with change. So if life transition is a psychological process, I bet you are wondering, *What part of my life will it affect?* It affects all aspects of a person's life.

In fact, Dr. Frederic Hudson found it will permeate your identity, confidence, intimate relations, family interactions, jobs, careers, social obligations, and ultimate concerns. Starting anew involves a move from a relatively stable time in your life to a fairly unstable time and then circles back to a stable time again. The stable period reflects time in the military. The unstable period reflects the outset of your return to civilian culture and the onset of the life transition process, which leads to a time of renewed stability and a new beginning.

Throughout this transition process, you will experience a range of feelings: anger, grief, sadness, and fear, as well as liberation, joy, trust, excitement, and enjoyment. The turning point toward stability is when you begin finding a new purpose and passion in life. It is about coming to terms with yourself. Once this happens, you can move forward to sustain the personal confidence and resilience essential to self-renewal.

Changing Your Perspective

Heads-Up

As you start anew, you will change the way you see yourself in relation to others and the world. Moreover, while the life transition will require a change in your attitude and behavior, it is also an opportunity for you to learn and grow.

Certainly you, like many who serve or have served in the military, take your role as protector of our country very seriously, and to be frank, your identity is defined by your rank, role, and rise to power and duty. There is a prevailing thought among many in military circles that members as a whole are more disciplined, honest, ethical, selfless, and courageous, are dedicated to something greater than themselves, and are just flat-out more principled than those in the civilian culture. Hence, military members often do not have high regard for civilian culture.

———————— Real People ————————

Ronald

"From my perspective, the civilian culture is a lot less disciplined and a lot less structured than the military. I'm not saying that's good or bad. The military is very disciplined. It's very structured. It has its standard operating procedures. It has specific doctrines, tactics, techniques, and procedures to accomplish things very efficiently. This is because they have to get things done in a very rapid fashion because, quite frankly, the defense of this nation and the lives of our young men and women in uniform depend on it. So over the years they have developed a culture of discipline, a culture of standards, a culture of procedures and policies that facilitate rapid, successful accomplishment of missions.

"In the civilian society there's not necessarily that sense of urgency, for a lot of good reasons. I think people in American society or any civilian society don't need that sense of urgency. If they want something to happen, they can take a week or two to do it and everybody is fine with that.

"I experienced a change in the work environment culture, going from a culture of a great deal of discipline to a culture that's less disciplined. That's one of the things about the culture of an organization where they call everybody by their first name, they don't necessarily knock on your door, if you have a meeting they show up ten minutes late and don't think a thing about it . . . and there's not a lot you can do about that, because that's the culture and the culture is much larger than you, so you have to adapt to it!"

When returning to civilian society from the military, because of the incongruence of cultures, you will be compelled to be more introspective and experience a growing awareness that the culture is much larger than you are. The vast level of authority, power, status, and privilege you were accorded in the military based on your rank, position, and respect have to be earned all over again, not to mention that title and position are no longer mounted on your attire—such distinctions are now invisible. You have to begin "unbolting" many of the things attached to your old identity that simply are not beneficial to hold on to in civilian life. You need to interact with others in a more meaningful way rather than looking at them as "civilians," because now you are or will be one, too! You need to be intentional about changing the things you can, accepting the things you can't, and being receptive to discovering the difference.

You need to maintain a positive attitude, trust in yourself, and be confident in your skills and experience. Believe that you are capable of adapting to and not only surviving in a significantly changed environment, but thriving in it. And if this life transition experience is going to have a reasonably happy ending, you bear the responsibility of influencing how you see yourself in relation to others and the world, adapting your outlook on life, and creating the desired result.

DYNAMICS OF LIFE TRANSITION

As discussed, life transition is not a singular event. As a result of a major life change, it is a dynamic psychological progression that is a normal part of our lives and must occur to achieve a favorable outcome. Life transition is not one-dimensional; it does not evolve in a manner that resembles a straight line. Rather, it unfolds in a multidimensional fashion comprising a time of emotional and cognitive (mental) intangibles (the unseen)—questioning, seeking, and starting anew—commingled with the more tangible everyday routine stuff. This ensues by shaping a new identity and new beliefs and attitudes about the world. Ultimately this process culminates with a sensation of feeling at ease with yourself in relation to your new environment and outlook on life.

────────── **Real Research** ──────────

Contemporary and seminal research studies shed more light on this experience. Dr. Sharan Merriam and Dr. Michael Basseches, experts in adult education and development, respectively, suggest that life transition involves becoming comfortable with changes in terms of identity, values, behaviors, and social roles; they further propose that we must appreciate that all answers to what is occurring in life are fleeting in the face of new information, experiences, and relationships with other people.

DEALING WITH EVERYDAY ROUTINE STUFF

Throughout the duration of your life transition experience, you will need to deal with everyday routine stuff. This is the business, personal, or miscellaneous activity that you pursue on a daily basis. It may be work activities like writing reports, filing papers, checking e-mail, or traveling for business; personal activities like paying bills, balancing your checkbook, shopping for groceries, cleaning the house, caring for the lawn, doing laundry, attending to the needs of your young or even adult children, caring for pets, going to the bank, post office, medical or dental appointments, or the barbershop or salon; and miscellaneous activities like watching the news, exercising, shopping for clothes, or running errands. These activities do not take a break while you are trying to adjust to the nuances of a new culture.

Although none of this everyday routine stuff is particularly difficult, you still must deal with it on top of navigating the challenges of life transition in the midst of a cultural change.

───────────── **Heads-Up** ─────────────

As you go about the everyday routines in your life, the experiences associated with life transition will continue to uncoil. Be intentional and find a point of balance that works for you so that you will not feel overwhelmed mentally and physically.

HOW LONG WILL THIS LIFE TRANSITION TAKE?

Life transition unfolds in a very distinct and dynamic—but not definitive—fashion. Overall, the process is gradual, requiring months or even years. The time required will vary based on the individual's intention to achieve self-renewal. As discussed, life transition does not happen in a simple horizontal fashion; it is multidimensional. This element, coupled with an individual's qualities and unique situation, will influence the length of the process.

───────────── **Key** ─────────────

There is always a possibility that you will get stuck in one state or another, but you must be intentional and deliberate in your way of thinking, being, and doing in order to move forward in the process.

A Successful Life Transition

As mentioned previously, your life transition will be anything but static. To ensure a successful life transition, you have to lean forward and contribute a healthy dose of personal work. The following chapters will discuss eight elements that are critical to this process:

- Self-examination
- Reflection and awareness
- Cultural adaptation
- Identity
- Purpose
- Personal and professional growth
- A support system
- Self-renewal

Within these chapters, you will notice a number of key principles that appear repeatedly in the life transition process and will help you make sense of the experience. "Making sense" is more than just comprehending; it is a process of coming to terms with the new situation and attaching deep significance and value to your life-transitioning experience. Making sense of life transition is unique to each person and emerges from a lived experience. Moreover, it is your passage on this journey from the cobblestones of puzzlement to the macadam of starting anew.

Although your life transition experience will vary, there are still common threads for everyone who emerges from the military to begin their integration into civilian culture. Table 1 lists my ten principles for success on the journey from camouflage to pinstripes.

Table 1

Ten Principles for Success from Camouflage to Pinstripes
1. Preparing for the life transition
2. Shifting your way of thinking, being, and doing
3. Surrendering a lifestyle and profession you may always cherish
4. Visualizing the change you desire
5. Developing a self-realizing state of mind
6. Nurturing your job satisfaction
7. Embracing change
8. Being confident
9. Experiencing new freedoms
10. Developing a new outlook on life

———— Real People ————

Winston

"When it comes to self-discovery, I learned that I am very capable of adapting to a significantly changed environment. My ability to analyze my environment, identify the traits needed to be successful in the new environment, and then aggressively go after those skill sets has enabled me to be successful. I have learned that this process is a journey. It is a period of time in your life where you are actually doing as the name implies—you are going through a life transition. You are not going to get through it overnight. It is an evolutionary process: you gradually change, gradually adapt, and things happen rather slowly at times. You cannot put a stopwatch on it."

In the next chapter, we will look at the three distinctive, multifaceted states of the life transition process in more detail and discuss the importance of self-examination and awareness.

If you change the way you look at things,
the things you look at change.
—Dr. Wayne Dyer

Chapter Two

How I See Myself:
Life Transition, Part Two

──────── Real People ────────

Ronald

"Despite my feelings of uncertainty, I decided that after twenty-eight years of service it was time for me to pass the baton to younger energetic officers to do their part for our nation. The decision was not easy. I gave my time and in return I was given everything: stability, education, experience, life lessons, and the means to support a very good standard of living. I'm very much indebted to the US military and the US Army especially."

YOUR MARKETABILITY

Before we explore the three dynamic states of life transition, let us examine one aspect that should be considered early in the process of your decision to retire from the military: your marketability.

Many of you are middle-aged, and it may be necessary to recognize your lack of experience outside the military and assess the pros and cons of your return to civilian culture. As you begin approaching the twenty-year mark of your life in the military, you will need to recognize that if you want a second career, you need to begin preparing, planning, and considering your marketability in civilian culture. Doing so will provide you with a reasonable amount of time to explore your options and commit to a new career. The other point to consider is the financial impact of your exit from the military and how best to leverage your preparations and marketability in order to optimize your financial gains.

You need to start preparing early by thinking about what you want to do in life after the military. You may need to be more introspective, which involves moving to a level of awareness that is in essence triadic—encompassing a perceptiveness of self, others, and the environment. Here are some steps you can take to prepare you for your move into civilian culture:

- Start forming a support system
- Grow professional network connections
- Join professional organizations
- Engage in the community outside the military
- Seek counseling (career, psychological, life coach, or other)
- Purchase high-quality business attire
- Attain education, certifications, and new vocational skills
- Envision a future that extends beyond the military

─────────── Real People ───────────

Andrew

"Time flies when you have your nose to the grindstone. I looked up and realized that if I really wanted to have a second career, I had better get in gear. I was not getting any younger. I thought I would be less marketable because of my age and lack of experience in the civilian culture.

"When I give advice, I hammer home the idea that planning needs to begin three to five years ahead of getting out."

LIFE TRANSITION SET IN MOTION

Life transition is a natural part of living. It is set in motion as a result of a marker event. As discussed in the last chapter, in addition to being commingled with the more tangible everyday routine stuff, the life transition process is comprised of the psychological intangibles that unfold in three distinctive, multifaceted states: questioning, seeking, and starting anew. Progressing through all three states during this time is essential to wholly completing the process, although the lines between them are often blurred.

QUESTIONING

At the outset of this change, as you surrender your old life in the military, you will experience a state of questioning and confusion. This is in essence self-examination, a query of yourself and your decision to stay in, get out, or retire. Of course, for those of you who are still struggling with whether or not to retire, you are experiencing a great deal of anxiety. Even once you decide, you may wonder whether or not you made the right decision. It is an exceedingly tough decision that must not be landed on lightly. Once you choose, there is no turning back.

There is no textbook answer on the "right time;" every individual must take into account his or her own personal circumstances, and the "right decision" is relative to the person making the decision. For some, you will be forced to retire by the institution for a myriad of reasons, but often the decision is tied to a limitation on time, grade, and promotion opportunity. For others, you may realize after you hit a certain mark that you are working for a minimal pay increase rather than longevity pay, so why not get out? For still others, you may simply be ready to explore new vistas, passions, or pastimes. You will discover there are many more questions than answers. This is not a novel notion in life—right? However, for those of you struggling with questions, know that you have all that it takes within you to arrive at a place mentally and emotionally where you can relinquish your old way of life in the military.

 **Real People**

Winston

"Being a career military guy, I had a negative impression of civilian organizations and strong perceptions about how civilians operated. For example, I thought the only reason a lot of companies were around was to make money for themselves; core and company values were written but not espoused; 'standards of excellence' was a buzz phrase, and people were expendable and unworthy of grace. These things I did not necessarily ascribe to, but I knew I was going to be a part of it if I was going to be employed by a civilian corporation.

"I knew it was going to be different, and I was very concerned about this major life change. The feeling was not quite fear. It was uncertainty and anxiety; hence my hesitation about retiring from the military. With that being said, someone once told me, 'When it's time to retire, you will know.'

"I knew it was time. I made the decision and never looked back."

SEEKING

What invariably follows the initial flood of questions is seeking—a search for direction. This is a time of inquiry, searching and probing to discover who you were and who you are in relation to others and your environment. Moreover, it is a time of cultural familiarization, readjusting, surrendering to new ways of being, and experimenting with new activities.

As you move into civilian culture, more questions will emerge as part of this new search. You will begin asking yourself philosophical questions. Many of the questions will surface as you reflect on your life, purpose, meaning, and contribution in the new culture. Still more questions will arise as you think about practical concerns involving your daily life, questions like:

- Who am I now?
- What am I going to do now?
- When will I get over these feelings of fear?
- Where do I start?
- Why did I get out?
- Will civilians accept me in the community?

This search for direction is a time of uncertainty, doubting, probing, and challenging yourself to gain insight and answers to the myriad of questions that arise in your mind. You will have to look inward, assess your environment, and draw on your self-confidence, self-reliance, and strength of mind to adapt and survive in a different environment. During this time, there are a number of steps you can take to prepare you for starting anew:

- Rely on your support system
- Reaffirm the value you add to civilian culture
- Seek out purposeful employment that will bring you job satisfaction
- Experiment with changing your leadership style
- Employ lessons learned from the military
- Change your personal appearance; be mindful of choosing quality clothing and shoes, as well as a refined hair style—remember that first impressions are lasting
- Discover new freedoms
- Focus on appreciating and managing your financial security

--------------- Real People ---------------

Ronald

"When I reflect, the decision to retire was evolutionary. That is what this life transition is all about; it is your ability to go from one phase of your life to another. I do not think you literally retire, walk out of the retirement ceremony, and suddenly you have accepted your new role in civilian life. I know I did not do that, though I have accepted my life now. While the military was very good to me and I loved most of it and would not change that experience for anything in the world, I know that part of my life is over. I think I have made the life transition and started anew. I feel solidly embedded in my new life and enjoy it every day, just like I did when I was in the military."

STARTING ANEW

Trailing the state of seeking, in a rather "aha!" fashion, is a time when you are drawn to begin your quest to start anew. During this stretch of time, there is heightened illumination and you embark on taking control of your future; in the process you experience a sense of self-renewal (which I will explore in more detail in chapter 6). This is a state when you begin to feel a sense of and take actions toward detaching from your old self and military life, take charge of your daily life, and launch into the new culture with boldness and confidence. In order to start anew, you must be able to let go of the old state of affairs and progressively shift your way of thinking, being, and doing.

―――――――――― Key ――――――――――

Reaching your goal of self-renewal will reflect an achievement of a positive self-attitude, an acceptance of civilian life, an embrace of change, and an anticipation of a promising future.

―――――――――― Heads-Up ――――――――――

You can expect during this time that your view of yourself and reality will be challenged and changed. Whether you believe it or not, in varying degrees, you will experience changes to your attitude and identity. However, the inherent personal values fostered in your formative years before entering the military will tend to remain over the course of this life transition.

YOUR EMOTIONS

During this stretch of time you will experience mixed emotions as you exchange the military culture for civilian culture. On the one hand, you may feel discomfort, anxiety, intolerance, and surprise; you may feel that you are socially handicapped and may feel invisible or disrespected by others. On the other hand, you may feel a sense of liberation, happiness, goodness, and rightness. These latter emotions fuel your confidence in your ability to traverse the life-transitioning experience.

You must look at change as a challenge—or even a mission if you must—and embrace it! For those who have made the leap, this is a good time to reconnect with your spirituality to ease your fear—fear of decision, fear of uncertainty, fear of fear. In an excerpt from his book *Fearless* (Thomas Nelson, 2009), Max Lucado offers some very illuminating advice:

> Fear never wrote a symphony or poem, negotiated a peace treaty, or cured a disease. Fear never pulled a family out of poverty or a country out of bigotry. Fear never saved a marriage or a business. Courage did that. Faith did that. People who refused to consult or cower to their timidities did that. But fear itself? Fear herds us into a prison of unlocked doors. Wouldn't it be great to walk out?
>
> Imagine your life, wholly untouched by angst. What if faith, not fear, was your default reaction to threats? If you could hover a fear magnet over your heart and extract every last shaving of dread, insecurity, or doubt, what would remain? Envision a day, just one day, absent the dread of failure, rejection, or calamity. Can you imagine a life with no fear?

Put this major life change into perspective: you have already demonstrated that you have the courage, fortitude, and wisdom to contribute to a cause greater than yourself in the defense of our nation. Have no doubt that you can move out into the glorious debris of civilian culture and contribute even more. Make no mistake—your perception of self and the world will be altered. Being able to let go of the old state of affairs and progressively shift your way of thinking, being, and doing will elevate your comfort level in a new environment and illuminate a path of growth and discovery that is purposeful and meaningful to you. A self-realizing frame of mind and trust in yourself are paramount, because a lack of this understanding, coupled with fear, will chip away at your determination to succeed now and in the future.

─────────── **Real People** ───────────

Benjamin

"I think there may be two ends of the spectrum here. On one end of the spectrum, I would describe the life-transitioning experience as progressive acceptance. Over time, I learned that I made the right decision to retire and discovered there is life outside of the military. There is even structure and camaraderie in the civilian community. Make no mistake, it is different. Since it is not born of the same pressures that you face in the indomitable military cauldron, it takes time to grow and develop into this new culture. On the other end of the spectrum, others have described their life-transitioning experience as a light switch. They had their last day of active duty, waived a military retirement, and simply moved on."

When you start this journey, no one is going to hand you a "You are now wise in this new life situation" card. You will find that this is a journey of deep learning, and you must discover wisdom for yourself through self-reflection and self-discovery. This introspection will be transformative in many ways, and it will lead you to a new outlook on life and toward the ultimate goal of self-renewal.

SELF-AWARENESS

As you move to a new level of self-examination, you will become more in touch with your inner self and your environment. This examination of inner thoughts, feelings, and experiences will consciously or unconsciously result in a transformation of your identity and attitudes.

───────────── Key ─────────────

You have to make a conscious effort to be introspective, to be intentional in your thoughts, expressions, and behavior, and to spend time observing, listening, and trying to understand the civilian culture. Work on identifying your weaknesses and then engaging in activities that promote personal and professional growth. Be mindful of yourself, others, and the environment. You simply need to give pause to view the world in a different way.

The upshot of awareness is being mindful of your surroundings and finding a point of balance that puts you at ease with your new life situation. Awareness also involves being conscious of your way of thinking, speaking, doing, and being. A big part of awareness hinges on suspending your modus operandi—your old way of doing things.

───────────── Heads-Up ─────────────

Many military cultural habits are incongruent with civilian societal norms. In the military, you devote your energies, interests, and inner self to the demands of the military, and the military organizes your life personally, physcially, and emotionally. You must also be prepared to die upon order of the state; there is more restriction on your rights because of the resolute need for good order, discipline, unyielding allegiance, and duty in military operations. Beyond these generalities, there are a multitude of small differences—for example, the differing views of time and dress between civilians and military personnel—and these are summarized in Table 2. Awareness requires you to be intentional in your approach to these many differences, and that will pave the way toward a sense of self-renewal. Recognition of the adjustments you will need to make is one of the first steps toward successful integration into civilian culture. Awareness will allow you to be more open-minded and open-hearted as you go about your new daily life in a more deliberate and thoughtful way.

Like a rocker switch, some of you will be able to turn off your former way of thinking, being, and doing and turn on a new way of thinking, being, and doing. But to do this you have to be intentional if you are going to truly move on. You may see it as a dialectic between being and becoming; this is similar to an old adage by John Henry Cardinal Newman: "To live is to change and to live well is to have changed often." It can seem like the life-transitioning experience continues forever, but self-awareness and introspection can help you through this challenging process.

———————— **Real People** ————————

Harold

"I enjoy spending time out in the woods. It's a great place to think. I don't think I ever coined the term, but it is true: nature is God's cathedral. When you are hunting out there, it is you and you alone, and it is quiet. There are no distractions.

"I believe that critical thinking occurs as we either verbalize or write down our thoughts. Prior to that point, they are just jumbled up in our heads with all of the other background noise. Talking about my life transition helped me to critically examine and share some thoughts, feelings, and memories that I kept tucked away."

Journaling is one activity that may be helpful during the span of your life-transitioning experience. Journaling is a reflective and therapeutic practice that can help you understand your way of thinking, being, doing, and communicating. It is a conduit to release your thoughts and emotional expressions as you navigate the stresses of this life transition. It provides a nonthreatening medium to examine your thoughts and feelings and discover obscure insights about yourself, others, and your new environment. As a result, journaling in essence becomes liberating, a self-imposed therapy to hasten your personal growth.

Key

The idea here is for you to experience a growing awareness of your thoughts, actions, and encounters with civilian culture. This awareness will be instrumental to you in making sense of, paying attention to, and adjusting to changes in your life.

Visualize the Change You Desire

The life transition experience requires clearly visualizing how you see yourself in relation to your journey in civilian culture. Visualizing has long been a powerful approach for successful people. It will provide you mental pause to return to your past, but more importantly, it will give you space to explore possibilities for your future. Like sports, life transition is 10 percent physical and 90 percent mental. You will experience gradual change as you navigate this process.

--------------- Real Research ---------------

The idea of visualization is drawn largely from empirical studies on visual motor rehearsal. This technique is used extensively in applied sports psychology, especially for high-performing athletes (e.g., Olympians). In their popular research on mental skills and peak performance, applied sports psychologists Dr. Kay Porter and Judy Foster discuss visualization in a practical way. In essence, they suggest that when you imagine yourself doing something exactly in the manner you desire, it physiologically creates a neurological blueprint in the brain that reflects the notion that if you have been there in the mind, you have gone there in the body. This is why visualization is so meaningful and powerful.

In order to effectively transcend the challenges of life transition, I believe one has to continuously visualize being surrounded by the environment and circumstances one desires to yield.

Many contemporary motivational speakers also advocate the practice of visualization. For instance, Zig Ziglar contends, "If you want to reach your goal, you must 'see the reaching' in your own mind before you actually arrive at your goal." And Dr. Wayne Dyer echoes more of the same: "The use of mental imagery is one of the strongest and most effective strategies for making something happen for you."

Engage in intentional awareness of yourself and the differences you must contend with as you traverse the civilian culture, and then visualize the change you want to achieve.

Real People

Winston

"In the future, I see myself as a very successful businessman looking for an opportunity to change my life once again into one where I am no longer a senior executive or a businessman, but self-employed and doing something that I am passionate about. As the old saying goes, 'no longer working for the man' but working for myself and living to live again.

"I look forward to simply enjoying my life and doing what I want to do every day, a time without the enormous responsibilities of running a business, turning a profit, taking care of and ensuring hundreds of employees are getting paid and getting their health benefits. I see myself with a less-pressured, more relaxed, laid-back lifestyle, enjoying the fruits of my labor."

We do not receive wisdom;
we must discover it for ourselves.
—Marcel Proust

Chapter Three

Reality has Struck:
Changes in Culture

---------------- Real People ----------------

Ronald

"This adjustment to a new culture included new lexicon. I mean, you do not go into a corporate meeting and say, "Hooah, roger that," or "10–4, good buddy." You have to be mindful of your language to ensure that you are not coming across as a military man. When a group of senior military officers gets together, the things they talk about are always different than when a group of senior civilian executives get together. Having participated in both types of discussions, it illuminated the contrast in cultures even more and shaped my way of thinking, conversing, and being with others."

CHANGES IN CULTURE

This chapter will help you make sense of the significance that a change in culture can have for you and understand why the change from the military to civilian culture is considered a major life change.

There are hundreds of definitions of culture, but the definition that Dr. Edgar Schein, a world-renowned thought leader in organizational culture, tenders is the most holistic understanding of the concept. He indicates that culture is the accumulated shared learning of a particular group. This accumulated shared learning encompasses behavioral, emotional, and cognitive elements of the members—in essence, the total psychological functioning. Shared learning occurs when there is a history of shared experience and stability of membership in the group. Here we are discussing two cultures: military culture and civilian culture.

Heads-Up

Culture is a phenomenon that encircles every moment of our daily lives. Nonstop, it is being shaped and sanctioned by our social interactions with others. This is evidenced in military culture and, likewise, in civilian culture.

SOCIALIZATION

An individual who has been a member of the military and returns to civilian culture has lived in two very distinct cultural environments. In fact, once you situate yourself in the civilian culture, you will come to realize that the military is a place almost entirely cut off from civilian culture; to some extent, in the military you led a wholly enclosed, structured, and routine life for an extended period of time. As discussed briefly in chapter 1, this is a facet of socialization that is vital to gestating and preserving the military culture.

You have been completely transformed by socialization, which is a significant part of the military culture. This process involves a complete change of your identity, from who you were as a civilian to who you need to be as a military member to operate within a "band of brothers," so to speak. The military socializes you to become a Soldier, Sailor, Airman, or Marine.

--------------- Heads-Up ---------------

Although the military socialized you for the first life transition, it is up to you to resocialize yourself as a civilian, and the process will be especially challenging if you spent an appreciable amount of time in the military culture.

MILITARY AND CIVILIAN CULTURE

Some would contend that the military culture is a subculture of the broader societal culture. Regardless of where you stand on that debate, it is quite clear—as evidenced by the military's core values, norms, and beliefs—that the military is very distinct from the broader societal (civilian) culture (see Table 2).

Table 2

Basic Differences between Military and Civilian Culture		
Characteristic	Military Culture	Civilian Culture
Appearance	Strict clothing and appearance standards	Generally informal
Authority	Single, with a directive leadership style	Multiple; varied
Conduct and autonomy	Socialization (i.e., behavior modification); institution guides personal and professional growth and enforces standards of discipline but also takes care of all individual needs (food, shelter, clothing, transportation, entertainment, medical care, legal and religious counsel, and recurring pay	Free-forming
Economy	Sound economy, balanced employment, no income taxes, universal health care	Employment left to individual; unstable economy, with changing levels of unemployment; income taxes; limited health care, with insurance costs shared by employee and employer

Table 2 continued

Characteristic	Military Culture	Civilian Culture
Justice	Unique code of justice; trial by court-martial, in which the commander serves as judge and jury; can be tried for violations of order and discipline, such as disobedience to a superior officer, drunkenness on duty, misconduct as a prisoner of war, adultery	Civil justice under the purview of federal courts; personal and private sexual behavior not regulated; only light restrictions on freedom of speech, political activity, and right to unionize or engage in group protest
Life	Conventional	Nonconforming
Safety	Low crime rate, though high risk during combat	Elevated safety and security concerns
Society	Enclosed/isolated but close-knit	Open, community segregation
Structure	High	Low
Timeliness	Expected to arrive fifteen minutes early to an appointment	Varied
Values	Respect for authority and position, loyalty, honor, courage, belief in operating as a cohesive unit, holding civic virtue over individual interests	Varied

--------- Real People ---------

Winston

"It really set in for the first time when I stepped into the boardroom wearing a suit. I quickly realized that civilian life would require me to adjust to different methods, procedures, and a completely different culture in order to secure my success. The experience of changing cultures is more than the symbology of exchanging a uniform for a business suit and reporting in to my new civilian boss; it is the overwhelming difference that I felt.

"I quickly saw that the civilian culture is less disciplined and structured than military culture. That structure is needed because the defense of this nation and the lives of our young men and women in uniform depend on it. The sense of urgency that is instilled in servicemen is not needed in civilian culture.

"It was a dramatic change in the work environment. In going from a culture of a great deal of discipline to a culture of less discipline, I can tell you about some personal feelings that I experienced. I call it the 'hero-to-zero syndrome.' In the military, you are given a great deal of responsibility as a senior officer, and a great deal of respect is associated with that authority. In the US Army, as a colonel commanding five thousand soldiers, when I walked into a room everybody in that room stood up to the position of attention until I told them to be at ease. When I spoke, everybody listened—not only did they listen, they took notes because the boss was talking and they had better take notes because I was not going to repeat myself and they knew it. Everybody addressed me as 'sir'—'yes, sir,' 'no, sir,' 'sir, may I have a minute of your time?' When I was in an office, nobody entered the office unless they knocked on my door and asked permission to enter. When they entered the office they stood at the position of attention until they were told to be at ease.

"Now, that is the military culture. Suddenly I am in a culture where I have a junior information technology guy in blue jeans and a T-shirt walking in and saying: 'Hey, man, I understand you are having trouble with your computer. If you will get out of your office for a few minutes I will get it fixed. By the way, I have fifteen minutes to do it.' So, my immediate thought was, *Oh, my gosh! Reality has struck.* That is a huge change in culture."

CONFLICT

This different set of experiences fosters conflicts in the way you feel and how you behave as a result of being situated in a new environment. In essence, your cultivated way of thinking and being may run counter to the ways of the civilian culture. The conflicts you will feel are equally tied to many of the societal differences identified in Table 2, which correspond to adjustments you will have to make regarding your mental framework of camaraderie, brotherhood, established identity, structure, expertise, dependence, and leadership roles.

I have already pointed out that returning to civilian culture is a major life change. You will discover that this change from military culture to civilian culture will make you realize how unaware you are of your own feelings, convictions, and ideals. As a result of socialization—which, as we observed, is a process involving a complete change of individuals' identity, way of thinking, and way of doing—

many individuals who have spent an extended period of time in the military find they have deeply embedded feelings, convictions, and ideals that simply do not gel with how things are done in civilian culture. So, in essence, a successful return to civilian culture involves an awakening and reexamination of these perspectives and value systems in order to preserve what works and jettison what does not work in the new environment. If you do not consciously check yourself on this, you could be in for a long, uncomfortable journey, because civilian society is not going to shift its basic structure and values in response to your needs. The bottom line is that the values and customs connected to military culture are not only different from those of civilian culture, but at times are in direct conflict with them.

CULTURE SHOCK

Because of the differences in values and customs, you may experience growing frustration with the civilian culture—more than likely, you will have feelings of fear, vulnerability, irritability, or even a sense of being overlooked. Know that this is inherent in a life transition process. Some scholars describe this as culture shock, which is spawned by anxiety resulting from a loss of any tangible embodiment of social interaction that was once familiar to you.

———————— Real Research ————————

"Culture shock" was originally attributed to Dr. Kalervo Oberg, a world-renowned anthropologist, and subsequently other scholars jumped on the bandwagon. It is surmised by some that Oberg arrived at the description of culture shock as a result of observing individuals' inability to adjust to a range of social aspects of daily life and the ensuing confusion, frustration, depression, and emotional distress associated with moving to an unfamiliar culture.

Dr. Peter Adler, a social scientist, extended Oberg's concept of culture shock to transitional experiences, such as those had by returning veterans and those who change roles or occupations in mid-career. Adler asserts:

> Culture shock is primarily a set of emotional reactions to the loss of perceptual reinforcements from one's own culture, to new culture stimuli which have little or no meaning, and to the misunderstanding of new and diverse experiences. It may encompass feelings of helplessness; irritability; and fears of being cheated, contaminated, injured, or disregarded.

In this vein, Adler observed that culture shock is typically associated with negative effects, although in the context of life transitions, it can also result in a number of positive effects. In the context of your journey, these include:

- Cultural learning (discovering the fundamental characteristics of the new culture)
- Self-development (changing one's lexicon, conversations, or leadership style; an individual simply steps up and takes personal responsibility for learning and growth through the intentional practice of self-examination, reflection, and action)

41

- Personal growth (engaging in activities that heighten awareness; transform one's identity; enhance skills, talents, potential, and condition of life; and contribute to the achievement of one's goals and dreams)

Returning to civilian society is a major change in one's life situation. As Ronald expresses, "You adapt, I guess, you adjust; you become smarter in the ways of a different culture." While there are frustrations in life transitions, Adler notes that there is growth and development inherent in these experiences and situations that demand personal change. He discovered that a more intense degree of emotional effect is experienced when the life transition involves adjusting to a different environment of experiences. These different environments of experience are also what foster behavioral and attitudinal conflicts, which I discussed earlier in this chapter. I have found in my own research that through a growing sense of self-confidence and self-reliance, individuals tend to make successive changes over time to adjust to the civilian culture.

Adjusting to Civilian Culture

As mentioned, there is a very clear delineation between military and civilian culture. Exiting the military and returning to civilian life involves a process of adjustment and acculturation to the new environment. This process, which is gradual and involves successive changes, will inspire a continual awareness of self and assessment of your environment. There are physical, emotional, and cognitive differences in the new culture that you will need to adjust to.

———— Heads-Up ————

You will be faced with reconciling and adjusting your feelings about many differences between the two cultures, including attitudes about work and authority; ideals regarding clothing; respect for position and title; willingness to cooperate and to accomplish things without consensus; willingness to extend warm gestures and conversation to strangers; unity of commitment and core values; and appreciation for the value you add, given that you are not indigenous to the civilian and corporate culture.

Remember that, as discussed earlier in this chapter, you completed a process of socialization in the military, involving a complete change of your identity, way of thinking, and way of acting. A different environment will foster a clash in behavior and attitude. In other words, the change in environment will not only illuminate the differences in culture but, coupled with the life transition experience, will impinge on the awareness, beliefs, feelings, ideals, thoughts, and behavior tendencies that were fostered in you.

———— Real People ————

Winston

"When I get together with the other vice presidents of the company, we talk about the economy, price of gas, effect of the new administration on our business, tax issues, unemployment, and union issues. We discuss things that have a direct impact on Americans' everyday lives. Military issues are like what unit is deploying next or the challenges with getting Class I or Class V ammunition from Point A to Point B. These issues do not even remotely emerge as topics of discussion in the business sector. Clearly, something I took for granted is that your environment has a huge impact on your perspective. This I discovered as I endeavored to embrace change."

Embracing Culture Change

Some individuals dread change, some resist it, and others embrace it. Ultimately, if you change the way you look at the conflicts that emerge with a change in culture, the differences you see will also change. You need to embrace change rather than dread it, which means looking at the perplexing situations that arise in a constructive way rather than resisting them cognitively, emotionally, and physically. This is similar to what Dr. Wayne Dyer describes as shifting one's attitude toward life and jettisoning self-defeating thoughts and behaviors. Culture change involves being aware of and open to new norms, rituals, and traditions that in many ways will be incongruent with the rich traditions, values, and norms you experienced in military culture. You will discover that the shared learning and history you have with fellow military members does not exist for you in the civilian culture—yet. You will need to be mindful of this and begin to cultivate a new shared history and stability of belonging in a new way of life.

―――――― Real People ――――――

Ronald

"Once you retire, you adapt, adjust, and become smarter in the ways of a different culture. There is an old saying: 'You have got to be able to change the things that you can change, accept those things that you cannot change, and be smart enough to know the difference.' That is the attitude I have assumed. There are parts of civilian culture I have no power to change. There are certain things in my little world that I can change, I should change, and I have changed. I have been able to do that, and I think I have been pretty smart in knowing the difference between those two things."

It is not what you look at that matters; it is what you see.
—Henry David Thoreau

Chapter Four

A Major Paradigm Shift:
Identity and Purpose

IDENTITY

You may be wondering, *What does identity have to do with life transition?* Identity is the sense of who you are as an individual coupled with your role as a contributor to society; its meaning is rooted in culture. Your sense of self is important because it connects you to the past, the present, and the future—who you will become. Erik Erikson, a world-renowned psychoanalyst, characterized identity as the conscious and unconscious way you see yourself. Obviously it is best to operate in a state of awareness so that you are always in tune with shaping your identify in a positive and meaningful way.

———————— Real Research ————————

Dr. William Bridges found that before you can become a different individual, you must let go of the old identity, and this begins at the outset of the life transition process and continues throughout.

Throughout one's adult life, identity develops, evolves, and changes. Dr. Bridges asserts that an individual must let go of the old identity. However, this theory is true only to a certain extent. Identity and attitude will evolve as an individual becomes more aware of self, others, and the environment, and during this process certain layers of the old identity should be abandoned—but not all. In this evolutionary period of time, individuals need to shed those layers of the old identity that are incongruent with civilian culture, such as physical appearance, attachment to rank, stature, position, lingo, and directive nature toward subordinates. However, there are elements of the old identity—confidence, self-reliance, discipline, commanding leadership nature—that are equally advantageous to the individual's successful life transition in civilian culture. For many military members, a deep sense of commitment is part of their identity, and perhaps this should also be preserved—if it can be redirected toward something purposeful.

Real People

Winston

"On matters of self-reflection and awareness, I think my identity has changed significantly. I, quite frankly, identified myself as a military officer, both by the uniform I wore and the rank on my uniform. When I was on active duty, if somebody asked me who I was, I would tell them I was a United States Army officer and a Soldier. I was very proud of that fact. I am now a businessman and vice president in a corporation. This is a completely different identity than the one I had just a few years ago. From my point of view, my identity has changed.

"On the other hand, I do not believe my personal values have changed at all. My values, like I believe those of most people, have developed over years, and what was important to me personally then is important to me now. Now, my professional values have changed somewhat. When you talk about values, you have to differentiate between your professional and personal values—the values important to you as you execute your duties and responsibilities in the organization as compared to your personal values. Personal values are with you no matter where you go."

As you become more in touch with yourself and your environment, your identity and attitude will mature and adjust. When you become more attentive to what is going on internally and externally, you will move to a new level of self-examination, as discussed in the last chapter. By examining your inner thoughts, feelings, and experiences, you will consciously or unconsciously experience a maturation of identity and attitude.

You will have a sense that you must survive, but also a sense that you must *thrive* in the new environment—your new culture. Your perception of whether or not your identity has changed as a result of this life transition may vary.

——————— Heads-Up ———————

While your rank may have defined who you were in the military, it may stifle your attempts to settle into civilian culture, since people will continue to call you General, Colonel, Captain, Ensign, Chief, Sergeant, etc. It is up to you to reiterate to others and to yourself that you are no longer that persona. Many of you have tied your identity to your military uniform and rank, and for some in the military, these designators accord a vast level of authority, position, power, status, and privilege. You will discover that in the civilian culture, your reputation and privileges have to be earned all over again, since your rank and position are invisible.

Individuals become increasingly aware that while in uniform, wearing the rank of "general," "full bird," "chief," or other titles, they were identified as their rank by both military and civilians. While out of uniform, they often are still identified as their rank by those who knew them before retirement. While on one hand individuals will desire to retain the respect and reputation they had earned in the military, on the other hand they should deliberately detach from the old identity and role attached to their military life and strive to become more than who they were.

What is helpful to individuals in shedding the incongruent layers of identity is to be intentional in engaging in new ways of being and doing. These new approaches will help redefine their identities by reconciling the conscious and unconscious sense of who they are as individuals and contributors to civilian society.

The life-transitioning experience causes one to assess one's values and attitude, determining what fits with the current situation and the new environment (i.e., civilian culture). It is essential that you give pause to deep introspection, and it will become perceptible through a growing awareness that one's values (personal and professional) and attitude will change in varying degrees—however gradual. It is not wholly necessary to change one's personal values, though one may be compelled to attend to corporate values to some degree just by virtue of involvement in a business. This is due to the fact that the attitudes, behaviors, and values of corporate America differ from those of an individual whose attitudes, behaviors, and values have been shaped by and cultivated within the cauldron of the military.

———————— Real People ————————

John

"I find myself more and more divorced from that military high. I do not have the same attraction to go back into that environment. I am seeking out new environments, friendships, and social settings. What caused me to change this was looking for something that is more value added on a personal basis. It was a really gradual thing that occurred in which I found myself drifting into a new mind-set, a myriad of new things like a new way of thinking, lifestyle, attitude about people, community service, and career. Everything has taken a whole shift in terms of my outlook."

SHIFTING YOUR WAYS OF THINKING, BEING, AND DOING

In order to start anew, you have to let go of the old state of affairs and progressively shift your ways of thinking, being, and doing. This requires a deliberate process of scanning your environment and experimenting with different approaches.

Here is a list of steps that will help you make these shifts:

- Seek out help, whether professional or personal
- Spend time reflecting and attending to a growing awareness of yourself in relation to the civilian culture
- Embrace new freedoms
- Cultivate personal and professional growth
- Shift your manner of dressing, use of military lingo, and dialogue
- Adapt your leadership style
- Spend time validating the value you add in civilian culture
- Get in touch with your identity

You will experience a growing awareness that solving problems and getting things done in the civilian culture require an approach different from that of the military culture.

 Key

There is no doubt that you are going to have to deliberately engage in new ways of thinking, being, and doing to help redefine who you are in the context of civilian culture. When you interact with others, you want it to be in a meaningful way. This is to say, be intentional with your thoughts, words, and actions, and be mindful of how you view the world and open to shifts in this perception. Moreover, be positive and focus on what you want. You should observe and follow the footprints of those you believe have made a successful life transition. It has been often said and proven time and again that success leaves perceptible trails.

PURPOSE

———————— Real People ————————

Oliver

"It was difficult adjusting to the first year and a half. The question entered my mind a thousand times: *How can I contribute to this civilian culture in a way that can even compare to what I did in the military?* It really takes a different mind-set to get through that."

To find purpose in your new civilian role, you need to own the experience, taking personal responsibility for your way of thinking, being, and doing—yes, your thoughts, emotions, and behavior. Delineate and examine the things that bring you joy and those that incite anxiety. You will know what these things are because one makes you feel good and nurtures your sense of well-being, happiness, and peace within, while the other does not. Examine the weight of the scale; ideally the things that bring you joy, happiness, fulfillment, and peace should be weighted more heavily, and if they are not, spend time in introspection and explore ways to make it better.

To use another metaphor, an appropriate balance is derived from being in a smooth flow, akin to an airplane in flight. The flight is smooth if the air flow is smooth, but the minute the airplane encounters turbulent air flow, the ride gets bumpy—sometimes really bumpy and uncomfortable. So life goes as well. Finding a point of balance means you have to be intentional about jettisoning thoughts, emotions, behaviors, and situations that spawn turbulence and discomfort. It is up to you to create a balancing point, but it is essential to your well-being and energy of mind, body, and soul that you discover where it is.

————— Real People —————

Benjamin

"My organization was undergoing reorganization and restructuring when I arrived. We had some very big personnel challenges that we had to deal with. I was forced to learn and begin to find my way through. So I found those things that I was able to immerse myself in that really kept me busy and gave me those new vistas, those new things to learn. I think that one of the greatest things that the military services do is instill in you a desire for lifelong learning."

————— Key —————

Engage in activities that will help you through this fairly unstable period of time. Be confident in yourself and actively pursue those things that give your life meaning and purpose. Take the initiative to engage in self-study to increase your general knowledge about your profession. As necessary, acquire vocational training or even an advanced degree. Remember, learning is lifelong. If you stop constructive learning, you cease to grow in a meaningful way.

Strive for results that have the most impact, pinpointing what is meaningful to you. You will discover that being intentional, positive, and believing in yourself and your abilities will prove to be very beneficial during this process.

Also, be open to a little levity. Laughter eases stress and makes you feel good. Other activities that you may find helpful include:

- Beginning therapy, journaling, or both
- Trying Hatha yoga and meditation
- Reconnecting with your spirituality
- Indulging in the arts, music, and live theater
- Simplifying your life
- Taking a long tropical vacation
- Volunteering
- Engaging in pastimes, hobbies, and sports

NURTURING YOUR JOB SATISFACTION

———————— Real People ————————

John

"There was a time when I thought, *I have no desire to ever own my own business. It is too many headaches and personnel issues and that is not what I want.* I never would have envisioned myself as an entrepreneur building my own business, and now that is what I'm doing. There was a major paradigm shift somewhere along the way."

Job satisfaction involves validating your usefulness and worth to an organization. A very important aspect of job satisfaction is your leadership style. In corporate America, the authoritarian style of leadership tends to be less effective than encouraging employee action and gaining consensus.

Adjusting your leadership style across the spectrum while also integrating applicable skills and experience learned in the military will boost your job satisfaction because this approach will produce results.

———————— Real People ————————

Ronald

"I am actually on my second job now since I retired, and my first job, quite frankly, was not that fulfilling. I was beginning to wonder whether civilian life was all that it was cut out to be. Perhaps, I should say, I did not know if I was cut out to be a productive member of civilian society. Then an opportunity presented itself, as they often do in this life, and I took it. This was kind of an 'aha' moment for me. Yes, there is a role, a mission, and a purpose for me in civilian life. I can make significant contributions to a community and organization that is not military in nature."

BEING CONFIDENT

———————— Real People ————————

Winston

"I think my attitude was the most helpful thing. I declared: 'I am going to succeed.' I am by nature a very positive person. I believe that your thoughts often become reality. You have to have positive thoughts and be optimistic. So, I knew that things were going to work out; I just did not know when, where, or how. I have been extremely fortunate and very grateful that things have worked out."

The final key to finding purpose is building your confidence. Confidence involves having conviction while being self-reliant and self-assured. You simply have to own what you want and go after it, thinking smarter and sometimes working harder than the next guy.

────────── **Real People** ──────────

Ronald

"A major ingredient in attitude is confidence. My confidence is as strong as ever. I think it is high now because I have made a complete journey through the life transition process. I have achieved renewal and established a new stage in my life. Quite frankly, as I was going through the life transition, I did not have the level of self-confidence that I have right now. There was much doubt in my ability to understand and subsequently execute the requirements of a civilian senior executive. Now that I have completed the life transition, I think I have regained the same level of self-confidence that I had while I was on active duty. Confidence is important to success in the military, business, and life."

What have I done with the garden that has been given to me?
—Unknown

Chapter Five

Go Out and Get It:
Growth and Support

———————— Real People ————————

Sherwood

"In corporate America there is no such thing as a free lunch. You are not entitled to anything. It is all about the skills, knowledge, and abilities you bring to the table. The approach du jour for measuring the cost of business decisions, investments, and actions is affectionately known as "return on investment." So one of the things I like to make people aware of is that in the military, you have positional and job responsibility. In civilian society, it is completely job responsibility. So in essence, your position is attained based on how well you are able to do the job and whether your performance indicates a favorable return on investment for the business."

TAP Revealed

What do you think the Transition Assistance Program (TAP) is for? I bet you are thinking that the Department of Defense's (DoD) TAP is supposed to assist you with resocialization back into civilian culture. Not so fast. The bottom line is that TAP is primarily an administrative program established to offer job search, career assistance, and related services to individuals returning to civilian culture. Its intent is to prepare you for your change from a military "career" to a civilian "career" and—in today's distressed economy—reduce the amount of time you could be on unemployment.

Real Research

The DoD policy does stipulate that TAP is "designed to complete the military personnel 'life cycle.' This cycle begins with the Service member's recruitment from the civilian sector, continues with training and sustainment throughout a Service member's active service in the Armed Forces, and ends when the Service member returns to the civilian sector." The informational literature indicates that the change from military life to civilian life is traumatic and stressful. It also tells you that some individuals are able to leave behind a considerable measure of their identity and find it easier than others to adopt new identities. It further advises that some will view this change as an opportunity to grow—that is, move toward reestablishing a new identity—while others will struggle with this change.

The bottom line is that TAP was not designed as a way to resocialize you back into civilian culture, nor does it empower you with the wisdom needed to confront this major life change. The onus is on you to chart your future and ensure your successful return to civilian culture. It rests on you to navigate the subsequent psychological process affectionately described as life transition.

—————— Real People ——————

Winston

"No one in this world is going to give you anything; you have to stand on self-reliance. One of the things my dad taught me when I was very young is, 'Son, in this life nobody can ever promise you anything. If you want something, you have to go out and get it yourself.' That mantra of self-reliance started when I graduated from high school and was able to obtain a four-year Army ROTC scholarship. That attitude has not changed since. I think that same attitude is what has allowed me to get through this very difficult life transition process and subsequently accept my life in civilian culture, and hopefully I will continue to be a success."

Personal and Professional Growth

—————— Real People ——————

Sherwood

"Vocationally, I will need to spend approximately $10,000 to elevate my knowledge and skills to the level needed to use basic Microsoft software applications, to learn typing, and even to learn how to use FedEx. These are things that are routinely used in the civilian workplace. I found the biggest challenge that people returning to the civilian culture have is a deficit in vocational skills. So when counseling other people in a similar situation, I spend some time on that."

A focus on personal and professional growth involves transformative learning, education, and self-improvement. This means reexamining your beliefs and experiences of the past to establish their compatibility with your present and future. It may mean obtaining special skill sets—whether managerial, technical, analytical, linguistic, or vocational—or studying a new business. It is simply ensuring that you are developing a level of sophistication and intellect that allows you to feel comfortable in your new environment. While some of the lessons learned in the military are useful, many are not transferable to a civilian occupation, especially at the more senior levels of corporations. This means you will need to acquire new knowledge and skills that are competitive with your civilian peers. You may find that you will need to spend a significant amount of time studying and conversing with others in your chosen industry to cultivate your business intelligence and acumen.

————————————— Key —————————————

Your personal values may remain relatively unchanged, but your views and values regarding business will in all likelihood change. This is because corporate values may run counter to values espoused in military operations. Quite frankly, you are going to have to cultivate your own personal and professional growth by reading and studying business materials, seeking out advice from mentors, observing and listening to business peers, and mindfully and deliberately engaging in new ways of being. You will need to change your lexicon, read literature appropriate to your field, engage in business conversations in an informed way, slow down your daily tempo, and shift your way of thinking and leadership style.

Real People

Ronald

"How to execute your responsibilities as a leader will be one of your most challenging feats. That is because a much different leadership style is required in civilian culture than in military culture. In the civilian culture, barking out orders and expecting them to be accomplished will not work. You have to tell people what you want done, usually why you want it done, and when you want it done, and then encourage them to get it accomplished. This approach runs counter to the military style of leadership, which is more directive in nature."

Resources

Real People

Winston

"Mentally, I had to take on educating myself in certain skill sets and knowledge that I had not gained through my experience in the military or the military education system. The bottom line is I knew that some of the required knowledge to be a senior executive of a civilian corporation was much different than being in a military organization. So, mentally I had to make a significant adjustment to those new requirements. I spent countless hours studying. I also spent a lot of time dialoging with individuals in the business world, listening, learning, developing and implementing new policies and procedures, and learning new techniques. It has been very good for me. I liken it to exercise; it is just as good for your mind as it is for your body."

The most phenomenal resource recommended and for centuries considered the locus of vast knowledge is the public library and the librarians who are there to assist you with unbundling, probing, and synthesizing a myriad of information. As a result of the digital age, I think our society tends to view libraries as an artifact of Nippur and Nineveh. Yet, like a rare jewel, a library's worth is what knowledge is to those who seek and crave it—priceless! A library is a vast collection of not only books, magazines, and newspapers, but a wealth of resources—computers, Internet access, Wi-Fi, printing, copying, conferencing, telephones, audio and visual supplies (e.g., maps, artwork, prints, historic and contemporary documents, microfiche, and microfilm), audio tapes and cassettes (believe it!), videotapes, DVDs, CDs, Blu-ray, video games, e-books, audio books, and services that can be exceedingly helpful for individuals exploring vocational training, self-study, or lifelong learning.

With that said, here is a list of motivational books that I believe would be particularly helpful to you on your journey from camouflage to pinstripes. These are simply other insightful perspectives primed to encourage, enlighten, and motivate you to embrace change, view boundaries as possibilities, visualize yourself fulfilling your potential, and create a purposeful and extraordinary new life!

1. Doubt is a traitor to faith. When you need encouragement to conquer your fear, try *Fearless* by Max Lucado (Nashville: Thomas Nelson, 2009).

2. Run at life with high intention. Rather than thinking of intention as something you do, think of it as energy that you are a part of and can draw on to cocreate your new life. Read *The Power of Intention: Learning to Co-create Your World Your Way* by Dr. Wayne W. Dyer (Carlsbad, CA: Hay House, 2010).

3. While you are on the journey of discovery and re-orientation, life can become quite hectic and stressful. It's important to establish margins to balance work and play and to establish healthy relationships. If you want practical insights on how to do so, pick up *Making Room for Life: Trading Chaotic Lifestyles for Connected Relationships* by Randy Frazee (Grand Rapids, MI: Zondervan, 2003).

4. Are you striving for happiness? Of course you are—we all are. Yet happiness is determined more by your state of mind than by external conditions, circumstances, or events. Explore a profound point of view on reshaping your attitude and outlook about happiness by reading *The Art of Happiness* by the Dalai Lama and Howard C. Cutler, MD (New York: Riverhead Books, 1998).

5. You know you are an expert at saluting and extending common courtesy, but if you really want a crash course in good old-fashioned manners, etiquette, and genuine hospitality, try *Social Graces: Manners,*

Conversation, and Charm for Today by Ann Platz and Susan Wales (Eugene, OR: Harvest House, 1999).

6. You will begin to hear a lot about being effective in attaining goals. If you are interested in a holistic, timeless, principle-focused approach to solving personal and professional problems, try *The 7 Habits of Highly Effective People* by Stephen R. Covey (New York: Free Press, 2004).

7. You were socialized to value honor, loyalty, and bravery, but how do you feel about personal accountability? If you are looking to fulfill your vision and goals, be viable in the marketplace, and take ownership of problems, read *The Question Behind the Question* by John G. Miller (New York: G.P. Putnam's Sons, 2004).

8. If you need reinforcement and common-sense advice on the importance of personal responsibility in your new personal and professional way of life, try *A Message to Garcia and other Essays* by Elbert Hubbard (New York: Little Leather Library Corporation, 1921).

9. Perhaps you are moving into the glorious debris of the business world. If you are interested in discovering the measure of a successful executive, pick up *The Effective Executive: The Definitive Guide to Getting the Right Things Done* by Peter F. Drucker (New York: Collins, 2005).

10. When you need a boost in attitude and a jolt of confidence about building wealth, try *Think and Grow Rich* by Napoleon Hill (New York: Fawcett Crest, 1983).

———————— Real People ————————

Benjamin

"You will have to go the extra mile to impart, perhaps even deluge yourself, with knowledge! Ask powerful questions of yourself and others that may arouse thoughts, trigger a response, or inspire action. Developing knowledge and the art of inquiry is simply a function of lifelong learning—and this they do teach and cultivate in the military."

Developing a Support System

———————— Real People ————————

Winston

"While you are going through this life transition, you have to take the initiative and seek out help. I could count the number of people on one hand who actually volunteered to help me. Fortunately, I am not shy or an introvert. I am a type-A kind of guy. I did not give a second thought to reaching out and talking to people who went through this life transition and had greater insights and experience about the civilian culture. The bottom line is that I took it upon myself to ask a lot of people questions: What is it like? How do you succeed? What is the best way to do this or that in civilian culture?

"More importantly, I think in life you have to find your heroes, role models, and mentors. I have a few; Ronald Reagan is one of my heroes. Whether they are people you know or not, you can glean their best attributes. I have been fortunate enough to also have several role models and mentors who I can bounce ideas off and ask questions of. I have actively listened, and they have given me some very sage advice."

A support system consists of advocates who constructively support and aid you in coping with the life transition. Invite your spouse, significant other, children, and friends to get involved in this life transition journey, and spend time with business peers and company executives. This group of individuals can serve as mentors to provide invaluable personal and professional advice. Seek out companies that have established support systems for members who have retired from or been former members of the military. You will need someone within the company who is willing to be a mentor, tuck you under his or her wings, and show you how things are done. Having people in the organization who understand what you are experiencing as a result of this change in culture will be instrumental in helping you traverse the life transition experience. The support system is a mechanism to help you through this fairly unstable period of time. What your advocates cannot do is visualize and be intentional for you—this you must do yourself.

I discussed earlier the importance of confidence and the need to have conviction and be self-assured. Some individuals carry these traits with them from their time in the military. Even without the support system, I think individuals of this caliber ("failure is not an option" types) can successfully navigate the life transition process. The support system simply adds an element of emotional encouragement, certainty, stability, and structure to the journey.

─────────── **Real People** ───────────

Oliver

"Spending time with my family and friends has been very helpful to me. Many of my friends are retired, and some are set to retire. So I have been talking to those who have experienced this major life change and those who have yet to experience it. Having a support network of family, friends, and advisors has been very therapeutic.

"Because I have been through this life transition, I have offered insights about this process to my friends who have to make a decision to retire or not within a year. It has been a very poignant experience. I have recovered emotionally and settled into my new life. Without my support network, this change would not have been a smooth landing."

*Take the first step in faith. You don't have to see
the whole staircase, just take the first step.*
—Martin Luther King Jr.

Chapter Six

Improvise, Adapt, and Overcome:
Self-Renewal

SELF-RENEWAL

Ultimately you will want to arrive at a place in your life where you have disconnected from the old situation and connected to the new. In essence, this involves shedding incongruent attachments to past ways of thinking, doing, and being and replacing them with new ways that are meaningful to you. I know what many of you are thinking: nothing may ever be as glorious as life in the military. The point of self-renewal is not about seeking something that competes with that, but rather coming to terms with the reality that life is no longer the same as it once was. You must engage in your life transition and be receptive to turning the page to a new you and a new life. We all look at life's journey in varying ways, but the difference lies in how we make sense of it and respond to it.

--------------------------------- Key ---------------------------------

You need a profound and powerful belief in yourself and a determination to do well in the civilian culture. What emerges is a growth of cognizance and perception, purposeful thinking, and an understanding of yourself in relation to others and your environment. It is clear that ultimately you will need a strong desire to reach a point in your life where you have detached from the old situation and attached to the new.

On the one hand, self-renewal means migrating from an old and unconstructive situation to a new and constructive situation; on the other hand, it means learning from each situation so that you can look toward a new outlook on life. Self-renewal is an inner and outer transformation. It is a shaping and taking hold of your life transition journey.

Self-renewal is a contemplative and gradual process of starting anew that cannot be rushed, and it consists of the actions and processes I have touched on in the previous chapters. This is to say, self-renewal is a continual process that occurs over time and will require embracing change, adapting to challenges, committing to your beliefs, connecting to your new environment, spending time in solitude to ponder your life, and asking questions of yourself and insisting on thoughtful and actionable answers. Moreover, the journey to self-renewal will require learning about yourself and gaining new insights that help you shed old habits that are not advantageous to your well-being or starting anew in civilian culture.

--------- **Real People** ---------

Omar

"Embracing change has meant experiencing new freedoms I had not experienced before. For example, the military has a rigorous work schedule and long hours. Going to work at 6:00 a.m., working until 8:00 p.m., and being consistently busy the entire time was routine. In the civilian culture, that is not necessarily expected. You go to work at 9:00 a.m. and for the most part everyone works eight hours and calls it a day. Most of the time they are working hard, but then they go home. There is generally no working on weekends, and certainly no one is deployed. I found myself with a lot of time on my hands that I did not have before. You begin asking yourself: *Well, what am I going to do with this extra time?* Figuring out what to do with my new spare time was one more adjustment I had to make."

EMBRACING CHANGE

Embracing change involves experiencing new freedoms and having more free time. It involves having a sense of financial security and making enough money to maintain the lifestyle you desire. It involves being intentional in exploring new ways of being—observing, listening, and understanding a new culture, and using a new lexicon and language. It involves being intentional in committing to self-reflection and building a sense of awareness: pondering your life, asking questions of yourself, and insisting on answers from yourself. Lastly, it involves your own self-discovery, learning about yourself and gaining new insights about the people and environment you must coexist with. You must be intentional and embrace the life-transitioning experience. Do not fear it. You cannot go back, so look ahead and welcome the change!

—————— Real People ——————

Ronald

"Embracing change meant I had to be intentional about new ways of being. I started out with the philosophy that I was just going to keep my mouth closed, my ears and eyes opened, and just see what this new culture held. But all the while I was thinking, *Man, things are broken around here,* or *Boy, things could be a lot better if they would only do this or if there was a policy for that.* I also tended to ask myself a lot of questions: *Why is the boss not saying something about this? Why is he not ensuring that people get this in on time? Why is he accepting these excuses?* I won't say I was upset about it, but it was just like, *Wow! I do not understand why they are not doing certain things.*

"I went through that period of questioning and then a period of embracing change. This meant I had to adapt and be intentional about new ways of being. I came to realize that things in the civilian culture do not require the sense of urgency that they do in the military. This is just the way things are done. Also, it turned out to be advantageous, especially while trying to learn a new business. I was not under the pressure to get things done yesterday, and I had time to absorb and learn a new way of doing things."

A SELF-REALIZING STATE OF MIND

There is no sign-up sheet for life transition; it occurs involuntarily. But it is up to you to shape the outcome. A successful outcome hinges on your frame of mind. In particular, you must develop a self-realizing frame of mind. This involves an awakening, perhaps of a spiritual nature; it is a manifestation of attaining happiness, freedom, and independence (in all aspects—cognitively, emotionally, financially, etc.). This is a state in which you seek to achieve success in all areas of life, including:

- Good health
- Financial wealth
- Professional and job satisfaction
- Tolerance, patience, and understanding
- Self-knowledge
- Healthy personal and professional relationships

────────────── Key ──────────────

You must employ the complete scope of your experiences and make full use of your talents and strengths to move through the life transition and navigate a culture change. Because the life transition process unfolds gradually, you will need to be contemplative and open to dynamic change.

Of course you can expect to experience a myriad of good and bad feelings and situations during your life-transitioning journey. However, this is where you step back and examine your identity, values, and attitudes in relation to your new environment. In doing this you will cultivate a growing awareness, self-reflection, and perceptiveness of yourself in relation to others and to your environment. You will find that basic survival and physical comfort are significant components of a successful outcome in this new culture.

SURRENDERING

If you expect to arrive at a place of self-renewal and have a balanced and satisfying life, it is important that you surrender to new ways of being and experiment with new activities. Part of surrendering is being self-motivated to let go of your identity connected with the military culture and move to embrace differences in civilian culture. This will foster a new identity, a growing sense of self, an understanding of your role in interacting with the civilian culture, an appreciation for a new beginning, and a constructive outlook on life.

Surrendering involves coming to terms with the idea of exchanging one way of life for another. Surrendering can involve aspects such as deciding to retire, adopting a different mind-set, and even changing your personal appearance and style and quality of clothing.

Your daily engagement with the change in culture will incite an array of positive and negative feelings. In all likelihood, you will miss the camaraderie, brotherhood, and military ethos that you experienced in the military, but you may also experience a sense of excitement, joy, liberation, and a resolute strength of mind to adapt and survive in a different environment. Surrendering involves reconciling your feelings through the process of self-discovery.

Real People

Winston

"Then there is the whole appearance thing you have to consider surrendering to. Do I really have to think about long hair, business clothing, etiquette, and not having mandatory fitness requirements? What planet is this? When needed, I was used to wearing the standard blue blazer, gray dress slacks, and a cheap white shirt that I purchased back in the days of Sears and Roebuck. Dropping my Class-A uniform, camouflage uniform, boots, and chloroforms off at the Salvation Army for whirlwind shopping at an affluent men's store to purchase expensive suits, ties, shirts, and shoes was a huge deal. Reality set in that I was not in the military anymore. So I committed myself to looking the part to better assimilate into the civilian culture. But what I have not let go of is a physical fitness training regimen. I think maintaining physical conditioning is paramount to sustaining good health, whether in a military or civilian culture."

As you have no doubt noticed, many of these necessary processes for a successful life transition are connected to one another; surrendering is tied to both awareness and self-renewal. It is about seeing the world in new and different ways and being mindful about paying attention.

Real Research

Along with his colleagues, Dr. Peter Senge, a professor at MIT Sloan School of Management, asserts that awareness requires suspension of habits and removing ourselves from habitual streams of thought (especially thoughts that breed counterproductive energy and actions). This awareness will allow you to be more receptive to what is unfolding in your life-transitioning experience and to operate from a more thoughtful inner place.

Surrendering is, in essence, letting go of the old way of life, stepping into the presence of a different sense of self, and starting anew. You have to be receptive to even begin to learn and grow from this experience. As I mentioned before, you want to ultimately arrive at a place in your life where you have disconnected from the old situation and connected to the new. This is the path to self-renewal, which requires you to learn how to move from situations considered negative to those considered positive. In doing so, you will surrender your eclipsed life and strive to create a new one that flows and flourishes in your new civilian environment.

A New Outlook on Life

———— Real People ————

Ronald

"I have a much different perspective on all areas of life now than I did while I was in the military. When you read the paper, watch the news, or go on the Internet, you find yourself reading and listening to things with a different perspective and maybe paying a little bit more attention to certain areas than you would have when you were in uniform."

Gaining a new outlook on life involves being solidly embedded in a new life and looking ahead. You have to visualize what you desire and think big. You have to open your mind's eye and believe that you can do more than what you think you are capable of doing in the civilian culture. Yes, this is easier said than done, but it simply begins with a vision, setting and believing in your goals, and taking the first step. Perhaps you desire to downshift, relax, unwind, and enjoy your life. Perhaps you desire to run a company. Maybe you can do it better and bigger than the current guy in charge. Whatever it is, see it, believe it, and go for it!

———— Real People ————

Winston

"One of my favorite characters of all time is a character in the movie *Heartbreak Ridge*. Clint Eastwood played the part of Gunny Highway, and one of Gunny Highway's sayings was, 'You've got to improvise, adapt, and overcome, but you must accomplish the mission.' His point was that there are going to be hardships, uncertainty, and ambiguity out there, but failure is not an option. You must come out of this a winner. Embracing change over time and changing how I view the world has been fundamental to my continued success in a different culture."

———— Real People ————

John

"I thought big before, but that is nothing compared to how big I think now. I have opened up the aperture. The possibilities of where my new venture could go are sometimes overwhelming. This is way bigger than me, and I am willing to allow myself to be caught up in something that is bigger than me. It even excites me more to think what life is going to look like ten years from now."

The narratives from real people throughout this book are just a sampling of experiences from the lives of individuals who have made the journey through life transition. After years of shedding layers of your old way of being, you will naturally arrive at a place of self-renewal. You will need to experiment with different activities and seek out new surroundings and social relationships as you begin to let go of your "elapsed life" in the military and take charge of your daily life in civilian culture. Like the individuals in these narratives, in time you will grow to embrace the culture change and accept your life in civilian culture, but you must be intentional and active in shaping the outcome if this life transition journey is going to turn out favorably.

The Essence of This Journey from Camouflage to Pinstripes

The life transition journey from camouflage to pinstripes is a contemplative and gradual process spawned by a change in culture. This journey, in essence, is traversing the lived experience that unfolds with your change from military culture to civilian culture. You will discover that this journey manifests feelings of discomfort, disorientation, and misalignment with yourself, others, and your environment.

By the very nature of survival, you will be inspired to examine your identity, values, and attitudes as they relate to your new environment. A growing awareness of yourself in relation to others and your environment will emerge. It will require you to be motivated to let go of the identity connected with military culture and embrace the change to civilian culture. This change is certain to foster a transformed identity, a growing sense of self and your role in interacting with the civilian culture, an appreciation for starting anew, and the shaping of a constructive outlook on life.

As you progress through this journey, you will begin to reorient, regroup, and surrender to new ways of thinking, being, and doing. Having a support system, nurturing confidence in yourself, being proactive in learning about the craft of business you chose, enhancing personal and professional growth, and being mindful and deliberate about changing your way of thinking will help you to complete this journey. Moreover, attending to your inner self increases your awareness, self-reflection, and self-discovery throughout the life transition journey.

You could choose the path in civilian culture that aligns closely with the life you grew accustomed to in the military or choose a path of new vistas and discovery, stretching you mentally and emotionally. Whichever path you choose, being self-aware and intentional will make all the difference in your life-transitioning experience and the manner in which you are able to start anew in civilian culture.

This journey culminates with a sense of self-renewal. It is a process of inner and outer transformation. It is shaping and taking hold of your life transition journey. It is a contemplative and gradual process of starting anew. You will experience a host of emotions in this state—feelings of self-confidence, enjoyment, excitement, happiness, and fulfillment. The idea here is that you begin to let go of the life you have eclipsed and take charge of your daily life by engaging in self-reflection, engaging in personal and professional development, and boldly seeking out new environments and friendships in the civilian culture. Embrace change, accept your life in civilian culture, and visualize your future.

The military has enriched your life in many ways. It has provided you with an abundance of opportunities and experiences, such as new skills, education, leadership mastery, time-honored values and traditions, a spirit of unity, camaraderie, and many other sound and enduring tangible and intangible qualities. Only you can decide to take the first step to remake yourself and shape your desired outcomes in life. And you and only you can decide what you will do with the garden you have been given and how you will sow the seeds of meaning and purpose as a contributor in civilian culture.

—————— Real People ——————

Harold

"I would like to get back into public service again. I think the military is the highest form of public service, one in which you put the most on the line. Also, I can envision warm tropical breezes and salt water splashing across the bow of my boat. That is where I see myself in the future.

"I used to always joke that I never planned my US Marine Corps career past next week. So, I am 100 percent sure that I have not planned the rest of my life. At some point in time,

I will stop doing what I am doing in business and get into the not-for-profit arena or, perhaps, put a cape on like Underdog, Shoeshine Boy's heroic alter-ego, and travel the world to help the needy. I think there is benefit to helping out humankind. I would like to be in a position where I can do that and still have the financial resources to go on vacation with my wife and go pheasant hunting in South Dakota.

"I think I have started a new beginning. This is an early chapter in my new book; I have turned the page on the military chapter and am moving on. I have always advocated for doing away with rearview mirrors on cars, because it does not matter what is behind you. What matters is what you see ahead of you."

As human beings, our greatness lies not so much in being able to remake the world—that is the myth of the "atomic age"—as in being able to remake ourselves.
—Gandhi

About the Author

D r. Sydney Savion holds a doctorate of education from George Washington University in Washington, DC, with a focus on human and organizational learning. Her interest in life transition was born out of studying the interrelationships, actions, and reactions of individuals, organizations, and communities in order to understand and help them define and solve their problems. Dr. Savion retired as a commissioned officer after twenty years of distinguished reserve and active service in the United States Air Force.

Dr. Savion lives in the Hill Country of Texas and rejuvenates on the pure beaches of St. John, USVI.